Cherish Me Always

Teddy Bears & Warm Fuzzies

Antique
Photographs
of Children with
Stuffed Animals

by Steven Micheal Wikert and Mary McMurray Wikert

Published by Hobby House Press, Inc.
Grantsville, Maryland
www.hobbyhouse.com

*This book is dedicated to Robert Larson McMurray
whose loved ones cherish him always.*

Acknowledgements

We would like to thank the following people for their special encouragement, advice, and generosity: Jim and Janet Doud, Spencer Wikert, Virginia McMurray, Dr. Solomon Wikert, Dr. Jessica Wikert, Alan and Marion Wikert, Bob Wikert, Cindy Blow, Sherryl Newton, Craig and Anita Johnson, Mimi Dietrich, Karan Flanscha, Don Johnson, Susan Brown Nicholson, members of the Prairie Rapids Doll Club of Iowa, James L. Jackson, Laara Duggan, J.J. Murphy, Gary Ruddell, Sherry White and the staff of Hobby House Press.

Front Cover Photo:
3½in x 5½in (9cm x 14cm)
In this post World War I studio real photo postcard from Europe, a young boy poses in his sailor suit. He holds a white mohair teddy bear with Steiff characteristics, including the shadow of a button in his left ear.
Previous Page Photo: Fig. 1
3½in x 5¼in (9cm x 13cm)
This English studio real photo postcard dated 1917, depicts a toddler girl with a much loved teddy bear of unknown manufacture. With shoe button eyes, a vertically stitched nose, and tattered ears it makes teddy's gaze into the camera very appealing.
Back Cover Photo:
3¼in x 4in (8cm x 10cm)
This unusual albumen image of the early 20th century portrays a young girl with a camera, barefoot in the grass. *Sherryl Newton Collection.*

Additional copies of this book may be purchased at $19.95 (plus postage and handling) from
Hobby House Press, Inc.
1 Corporate Drive, Grantsville, MD 21536
1-800-554-1447
www.hobbyhouse.com
or from your favorite bookstore or dealer.

Printed in the United States of America

ISBN: 0-87588-604-3

Fig. 2
3¼in x 5in (8cm x 13cm)
Two boys pose with their unusual mohair animals in this studio real photo postcard with a stamp box dating to post-1918. Judging from their long tails, it is a possibility that one is a monkey and the other is a kangaroo. The boys' suits with sailor collar and shoulder side buttons are made of serviceable fabric.

Fig. 3
3½in x 5½in (9cm x 14cm)
The white mohair bear in this studio real photo postcard resembles those made by
the Steiff® factory in Germany around 1909. The toddler girl in her batiste dress
with bertha collar, points to teddy's black shoe button eyes, small cupped ears,
elongated arms with spoon shaped paws, and large feet with narrow ankles.

Cherish Me Always

I'm the object of love and care,
That warm and fuzzy teddy bear.

A century old I am today,
But still am loved in every way.

Roosevelt and Steiff did not know,
What they started so long ago.

I'm valued now because I'm old,
But past love was worth more than gold.

My image still remains these days,
So please, please, Cherish Me Always.

S.M. Wikert

Fig. 4
4¼in x 6½in (11cm x 17cm)
The thoughtful boy in this silver print poses with his handsome mohair bear.
Teddy's triangular face and footpads reinforced with cardboard are both possible
indicators that this bear was made by the Ideal Novelty and Toy Company of New
York during the first decade of the twentieth century.

Introduction

Viewing old photographs of children with their cherished warm and fuzzy possessions creates a special magic that has captivated both of us for over a decade of collecting. We have spent countless hours searching in a variety of places to rediscover the often abandoned and illusive image of the child from the past before it is lost forever.

Each of our photographic discoveries becomes a magical window into history. We are allowed to wander through time as we view and study each image that demonstrates the relationship between the child and their cherished teddy bear or stuffed toy. On a broader scope, we recognize that these photographs record this relationship as a prerequisite to becoming a good father or mother. The practice of children's play establishes the cornerstone for the family structure of today and tomorrow as well as for relationships extending outward to all humanity. Collecting these small bits of history allows us to marvel at how much life has changed during the past 140 years. However, these images also demonstrate that the needs for belonging, enjoying life, and giving love are enduring and untouched by time.

Examples similar to the images published on the following pages are often challenging to find. As more collectors are joining the search, finding excellent images becomes increasingly difficult and more costly. We feel there are several factors to consider when purchasing a photograph from the past: the type of image, the clarity of the image, the condition of the image, the rarity of the teddy bear or stuffed animal, the notoriety of the persons in the image, the aesthetic quality of the image, and finally the price.

We hope our sampling will give our readers an overview of the teddy bears, stuffed animals, and related clothing belonging to children of the past. Although positive identification of the photographic type is usually possible, exact attribution of a specific teddy bear or stuffed animal is not as precise. Without physically examining the toy in question, we can only research and point out visual similarities, which may suggest a possible provenance of a given maker. In some cases, the exact dating of the photograph is made very easy by referring to written dates, postmarks, and stamp boxes. When these are not available, approximate dates can be determined by style of clothing, photo presentation, and the various stuffed animals included in these historical portraits. Measurements listed with each caption pertain to the original photographic dimensions, even though the format and size of the image may have been edited to compliment this book.

Please refer to the Guide to Photographic Terms in the back of this book for help in identifying and understanding the various photographic processes, many of which are represented in this volume. The Selected Bibliography gives a list of sources that will offer more detailed information on photographic identification and processes as well as historical information about teddy bears, stuffed animals, and clothing styles. Attributions, when known, are listed immediately following.

It is rewarding for us to share these historical photographs and give them the attention they so richly deserve in this book format. We are truly thankful for the opportunity to be guardians of these photographic treasures during our lifetimes and we hope that these images will indeed be cherished always.

Mary McMurray Wikert
Steven Micheal Wikert

Fig. 5 (below)
3½in x 5in (9cm x 13cm)
This dated 1913 real photo postcard pictures
two children in their "bearskin" cloth coats of
the era. These mohair plush coats were made
very popular by the teddy bear craze, which
enveloped America during the period.

Fig. 6 (left)
3½in x 5½in (9cm x 14cm)
The young boy in this mid twentieth century tinted real photo postcard of French origin poses in his Sunday best suit. His large European bear of chocolate brown mohair looks attentively at his young owner.

Fig. 7 (above)
4in x 6in (10cm x 15cm)
The poke bonnet with double ruffle frames the face of this happy little girl in this studio silver print circa 1910. Her stuffed cloth squirrel companion is dressed in a stylish waistcoat and vest.

Fig. 8 (left)
3in x 5¼in (8cm x 13cm)
A toddler poses with her peeled banana in this real photo postcard taken around 1915. Nearby sits a teddy doll of unknown manufacture, an unusual example of a mohair bear body with a celluloid doll face. Teddy doll is ready for a ride in a wooden wagon pulled by "Pacing Bob".

Fig. 9 (right)
3¼in x 5¼in (8cm x 13cm)
A toddler girl smiles at the camera while wearing a white mohair plush "bearskin" coat in this studio real photo postcard circa 1915. Her unique fur muff has a purse on top. The stamp box design on the reverse side indicates a pre-1915 date.

Fig. 10
3¼in x 5¼in (8cm x 13cm)
A young girl in a white eyelet lace trimmed dress kisses a white mohair teddy bear of
European origins in this commercial real photo postcard postmarked 1913.

Fig. 11 (right)
3¼in x 5¼in (8cm x 13cm)
A young girl with a mohair teddy bear tucked under her arm glances up from her writing slate in this commercial real photo postcard. Her bow and dress from the 1920s are delicately hand tinted.

Hartelijk gefeliciteerd

Fig. 12 (left)
3in x 6in (8cm x 15cm)
A toddler girl stands next to a fully jointed mohair bear of probable European origins. The bear is seated on an ice cream stool in this studio silver print of the World War I era.

I like little Pussy,
Her coat is so warm
And if I don't hurt her
She'll do me no harm.
So I'll not pull her tail,
Nor drive her away,
But Pussy and I
Very gently will play;
She shall sit by my side,
And I'll give her some food;
And she'll love me because
I am gentle and good.

From
"I Like Little Pussy"
Jane Taylor

Willyerd, Bryan, Texas.

Fig. 13
4¼in x 6½in (11cm x 17cm)
The baby in this unusual albumen cabinet card of the 1890s hugs a large stuffed cloth cat. Various American companies marketed the printed cat's image on a sheet of fabric. The purchaser then cut, sewed, and stuffed the cat at home to make the finished example. *Jim and Janet Doud Collection.*

Fig. 14
3¼in x 5¼in (8cm x 13cm)
This English real photo postcard from the World War I era depicts a toddler with her jointed bear made of mohair plush standing on a Victorian carved straight back chair.

Fig. 15 (left)
3¾in x 4¼in
(10cm x 11cm)
A trio of children in white starched dresses of the pre-World War I era contentedly perch on stools in this studio silver print. Although the bear is turned from the camera, it is evident that he is fully jointed.

Fig. 16 (right)
3¼in x 5¼in (8cm x 13cm)
Brother and sister pensively pose in their white dresses before the camera in this studio real photo postcard from the World War I era. The bear with his large black embroidered nose resembles examples produced in England during this time.

Fig. 17
3¾in x 5¾in (10cm x 15cm)
This rather serious young boy holds his jointed dark brown bear in his lap as the studio photographer of this silver print records the event. His sailor suit and high button shoes are appropriate wear for a boy of the second decade of the twentieth century.

Fig. 18 (left)
3½in x 5½in (9cm x 14cm)
This charming hand-tinted commercial French postcard is identified as a "little chauffeur" wearing his real fur coat from the World War I era.

Fig. 19 (right)
3¼in x 5in (8cm x 13cm)
A stuffed mohair dog with spaniel ears and stitched nose and mouth comforts the barefoot baby in this studio real photo postcard from England. It was probably taken during the second decade of the twentieth century. *Jim and Janet Doud Collection.*

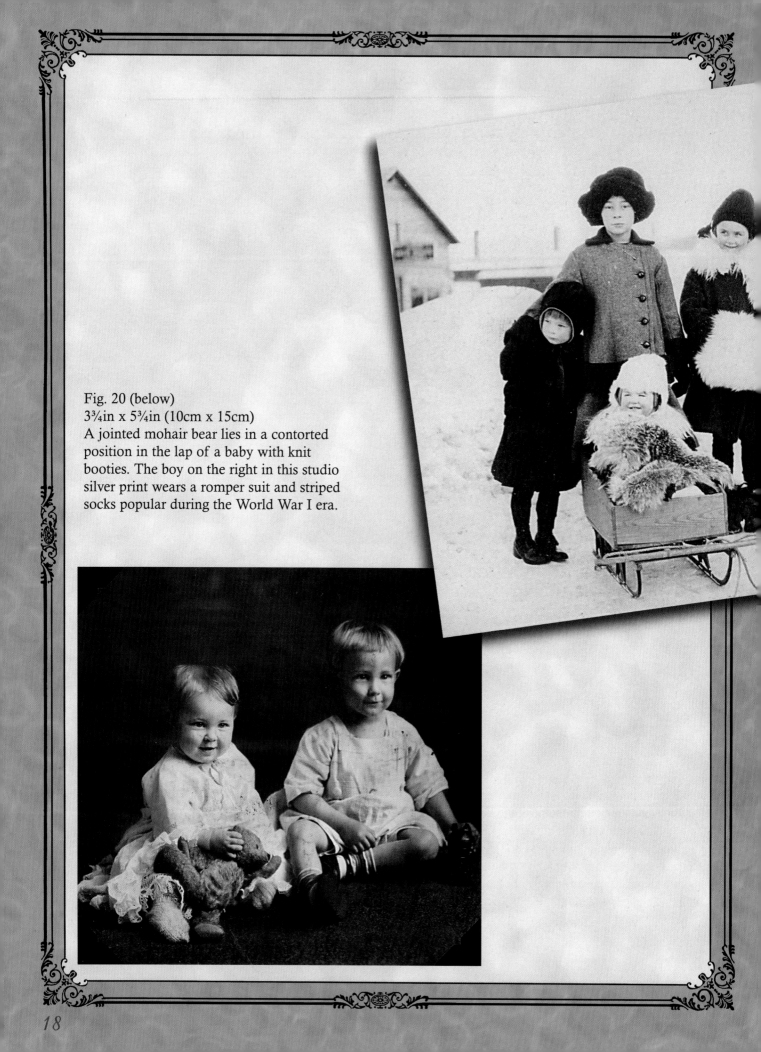

Fig. 20 (below)
3¾in x 5¾in (10cm x 15cm)
A jointed mohair bear lies in a contorted position in the lap of a baby with knit booties. The boy on the right in this studio silver print wears a romper suit and striped socks popular during the World War I era.

Fig. 21 (left)
5½in x 3½in (14cm x 9cm)
These seven girls are dressed for snowy weather in this real photo postcard from the second decade of the twentieth century. The matching muffs and collars resemble fox fur, while the curly muff is probably angora.

Fig.22 (right)
3¼in x 5¼in (8cm x 13cm)
A baby holds a much loved mohair teddy bear of undetermined origins in this studio real photo postcard circa 1915.

Looking Forward

When I am grown to a man's estate
I shall be very proud and great,
and tell the other girls and boys
Not to meddle with my toys.

Robert Louis Stevenson
A Child's Garden of Verses

Fig. 23
3½in x 5½in (9cm x 14cm)
A shoeless baby balances precariously on an ice cream stool while dangling a mohair plush stuffed animal with pointed ears. The stamp box on this real photo postcard indicates a circa 1912 date.

Fig. 24 (left)
3¼in x 5½in (8cm x 14cm)
This post World War I real photo postcard is a studio portrait of a toddler boy in his romper suit tightly holding his mohair bear.

Fig. 25 (right)
4¼in x 6½in (11cm x 17cm)
This albumen cabinet card shows a girl dressed in a cloak with a Mother Hubbard waist and pleated pompadour sleeves. She pushes a 3-wheeled doll perambulator containing a "Tabby Cat" that sold for 6¢ in 1894 in the *Montgomery Ward & Co. Catalogue & Buyers Guide.*

Patten Bros.   EXTRA FINISH.   Waterloo, Wis.

Fig. 26 (left)
3¼in x 5¼in (8cm x 13cm)
This white mohair "bearskin" outfit almost covers this toddler from head to toe in this studio real photo postcard. The stamp box on the reverse side indicates a circa 1910 date.

Fig. 27 (right)
3½in x 5½in (9cm x 14cm)
A young boy proudly displays his fluffy mohair plush teddy bear for the camera in this real photo postcard with a stamp box date of about 1910. His serviceable sailor suit with bloomer pants was a popular style during this period.

Fig. 28 (above)
3¼in x 5¼in (8cm x 13cm)
Postmarked from the Netherlands, this hand-tinted commercial real photo postcard of pre-World War I vintage shows an unusual mohair dog. His large side-glancing round eyes gaze at a girl all dressed in pink.

Fig. 29 (right)
3¼in x 5¼in (8cm x 13cm)
A serious young girl wearing an open neck dress with a white guimpe or blouse holds her bear closely. Her outfit is a popular style of the first decade of the twentieth century in this real photo postcard.

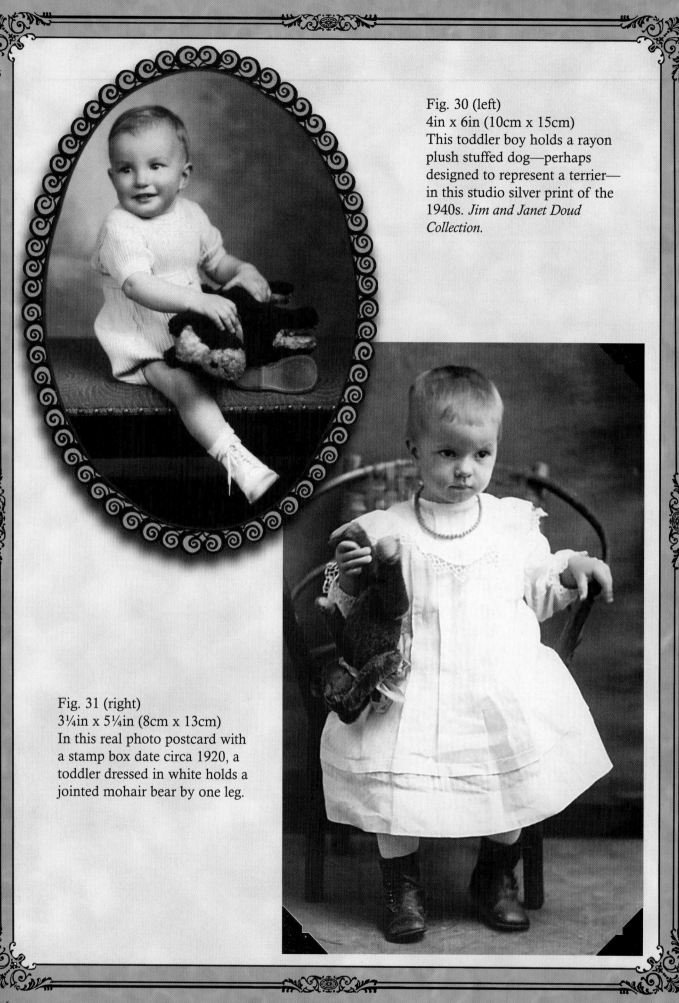

Fig. 30 (left)
4in x 6in (10cm x 15cm)
This toddler boy holds a rayon plush stuffed dog—perhaps designed to represent a terrier—in this studio silver print of the 1940s. *Jim and Janet Doud Collection.*

Fig. 31 (right)
3¼in x 5¼in (8cm x 13cm)
In this real photo postcard with a stamp box date circa 1920, a toddler dressed in white holds a jointed mohair bear by one leg.

Fig. 32
3¼in x 5¼in (8cm x 13cm)
In this postmarked 1912 real photo postcard, a lucky little girl poses in her
mohair "bearskin" coat and buttoned leggings. Her collar and muff are
real fur possibly of fox or china goat.

My Bed is a Boat

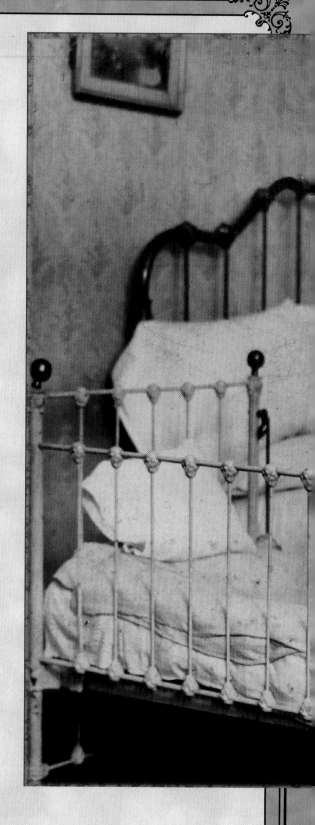

My bed is a little boat;
Nurse helps me in when I embark;
She girds me in my sailor's coat
And starts me in the dark.

At night, I go on board and say
Good night to all my friends on shore;
I shut my eyes and sail away
And see and hear no more.

And sometimes things to bed I take,
As prudent sailors have to do;
Perhaps a slice of wedding cake,
Perhaps a toy or two.

All night across the dark we steer;
But when the day returns at last;
Safe in my room, beside the pier
I find my vessel fast.

Robert Louis Stevenson
A Child's Garden of Verses

Fig. 33
5¼in x 4in (13cm x 10cm)
This silver print of a young boy with his teddy bear is both charming and unusual because the photograph was taken in an actual bedroom setting rather than in a studio. Both beds of cast iron are styles commonly found in the early twentieth century.

Fig. 34 (below)
2½in x 4in (6cm x 10cm)
A tartan plaid cape and dress accented
with a white fur collar and muff were
considered very stylish in this
albumen carte de visite from the late
1860s.

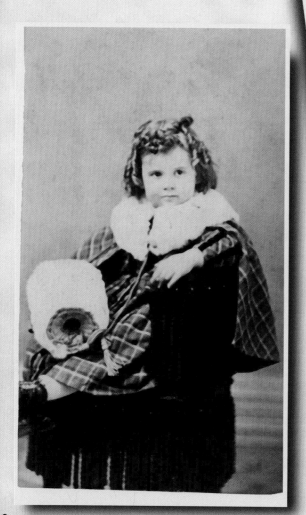

PARIS
1145

Fig. 35 (left)
3½in x 5¼in
(9cm x 13cm)
The three girls in this tinted French commercial real photo postcard are wearing dresses of the 1920s. The mohair bear is a less expensive model with white eyes. A fur poodle is posed nearby.

Fig. 36 (above)
3¾in x 5¾in (10cm x 15cm)
A baby dressed in white is perched on a photographer's ledge in this circa 1930 silver print. The mohair dog standing nearby on its hind legs has dark spaniel ears.

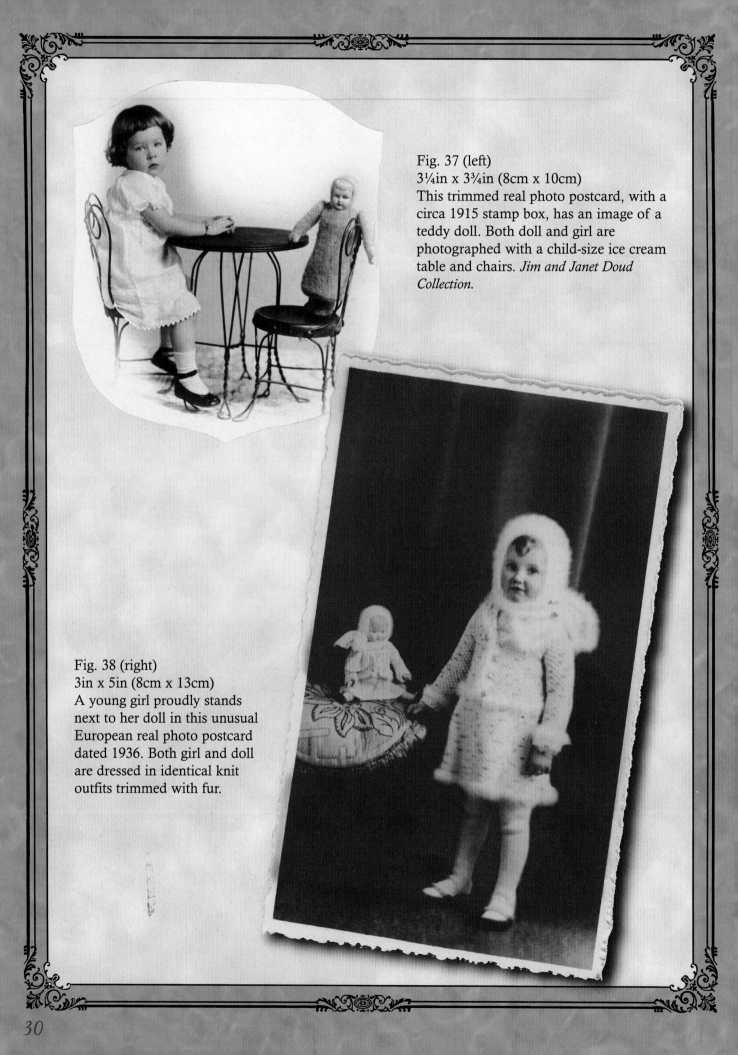

Fig. 37 (left)
3¼in x 3¾in (8cm x 10cm)
This trimmed real photo postcard, with a circa 1915 stamp box, has an image of a teddy doll. Both doll and girl are photographed with a child-size ice cream table and chairs. *Jim and Janet Doud Collection.*

Fig. 38 (right)
3in x 5in (8cm x 13cm)
A young girl proudly stands next to her doll in this unusual European real photo postcard dated 1936. Both girl and doll are dressed in identical knit outfits trimmed with fur.

Fig. 39
5in x 7¼in (13cm x 19cm)
Teddy has his back to the camera in this studio silver print. Judging from his
straight short limbs and sausage-shaped body, he may be an American "stick"
bear of the 1920s.

Fig. 40 (left)
3½in x 5½in (9cm x 14cm)
A fluffy mohair bear gets a big hug from a little girl dressed in overalls and a large straw hat. This informal studio image, circa 1910, is in a real photo postcard format.

Fig. 41 (right)
3½in x 5½in (9cm x 14cm)
These solemn sisters pose for this real photo postcard circa 1915. Their serviceable dresses with low waistlines were worn for play. Their mohair bear by an unknown maker was probably a favorite companion.

Fig. 42
5¼in x 3¼in (13cm x 8cm)
The large mohair monkey in this family group shot adds a
touch of whimsy to this real photo postcard with a circa
1915 stamp box.

...*G is for glad little Gustave,*
Who says that a monkey he must have;
But his mother thinks not,
And say that they've got
All the monkey they care for in Gustave...

From "Alphabet for Children"
Isabel Frances Bellows
Baby World, a compilation by
Mary Mapes Dodge, St. Nicholas

Fig. 43 (above)
3¼in x 2¼in (8cm x 6cm)
A toddler sets up his "Scout Express" wagon to give his teddy bear and two friends a ride in the snow in this candid post-World War I snapshot.

Fig. 44 (above)
3¼in x 2¼in (8cm x 6cm)
This image is a different snapshot view of Fig. 43 with a teddy bear and his friends on board the "Scout Express." The knit snowsuit is a typical style of the post-World War I period.

Fig. 45 (left)
4in x 3¼in (10cm x 8cm)
Identical twin girls dressed in white in twin wicker rockers gaze into the camera in this rare silver print from the early part of the twentieth century. One cradles a fluffy mohair bear and the other holds a bisque head German doll. *Jim and Janet Doud Collection.*

Fig. 46
4in x 6 ½in (10cm x 17cm)
This young boy is handsomely attired in a jacket with lace collar, vest, and a skirt with kilt plaits in this albumen cabinet card circa 1890. He carries a china head doll while a cloth stuffed elephant watches nearby.

Fig. 47 (above)
5¼in x 3¼in (13cm x 8cm)
A little girl and her giant-sized mohair bear enjoy each other's company in this vivid French commercial real photo postcard from the 1920s.

Fig. 48 (right)
2¾in x 3¼in (7cm x 8cm)
Although the case is missing from this tintype image of the 1860s, the brass matt and preserver (a thin frame that holds the image packet together) are beautifully embossed and compliment this uncommon image of a young girl and her doll. Both are dressed in hats and capes and the fur trim on the girl's outfit resembles white ermine.

Fig. 49 (left)
5¼in x 3¼in (13cm x 8cm)
A toddler poses with his menagerie of stuffed toys and one German doll. Teddy is smartly dressed in hat and coat. Cloth printed examples include "Tabby Cat", "Tabby's Kitten", "Foxy Grandpa", "Buster Brown", and "Tige" in this real photo postcard of the early 20th century.

Fig. 50 (right)
5½in x 3½in (14cm x 9cm)
A postmarked 1908 real photo postcard of a girl and her dark brown mohair bear was taken in an unknown photographer's studio.

Fig. 51
3in x 4in (8cm x 10cm)
In this studio silver print of the early 1920s, a baby in a fluffy fur coat with matching bonnet sits in a 4 wheel folding gocart. It is upholstered in simulated leather cloth.

Fig. 52 (left)
3¼in x 5¼in (8cm x 13cm)
A young girl dressed in a lamb fur coat lovingly cuddles her bear in this real photo postcard postmarked 1911. Her collar and muff are made of angora.

Fig. 53 (right)
3½in x 5½in (9cm x 14cm)
A young girl dressed in white happily hugs her teddy bear with a wooden lawn swing behind her. The stamp box on this real photo postcard indicates a circa 1912 date.

Fig. 54 (left)
2½in x 4in (6cm x 10cm)
This interesting carte de visite shows the image of a young child wearing a low-waisted dress with a double flounce skirt typical of the 1880s. On a ledge nearby is an unusual figure of a large owl made of undetermined materials.

A wise old owl lived in an oak;
The more he saw the less he spoke.
The less he spoke the more he heard.
Why can't we all be like that wise old bird?

Edward Hersey Richards

Fig. 55 (left)
2½in x 4in (6cm x 10cm)
The red lined border of this carte de visite helps to date this photograph from the 1860s. The girl's pelisse or cloak has a double cape accented with a trail-trimmed fur collar. She holds an elaborate fur muff.

Fig. 56 (right)
3¼in x 4½in (8cm x 12cm)
A toddler in a smocked dress of the mid 20th century stands near a bear probably made of nylon plush. Teddy has contrasting felt pads in this studio silver print.

Fig. 57 (left)
4½in x 6in (12cm x 15cm)
A little girl of the 1920s
hugs a fluffy mohair dog
with a black stitched nose
in this studio portrait silver
print.

Fig. 58 (right)
3½in x 5½in (9cm x 14cm)
A jointed mohair teddy rests on the lap of
this happy baby in his wicker carriage. This
real photo postcard has a pre-1915 stamp box.

Fig. 59 (left)
3½in x 4½in (9cm x 12cm)
Two toddlers, clad only in
diapers, pose for the camera in
this studio silver print dated
1921. One holds a stuffed
animal of pale mohair.

Fig. 60 (right)
3¼in x 5¼in (8cm x 13cm)
This real photo postcard, with a
circa 1915 stamp box, records the
image of a stylish girl in a curly
mohair "bearskin" coat with a
swirling pattern. Muff, fancy
bonnet, and trimmed collar make
this a stunning outfit.

Fig. 61
3¼in x 5¼in (8cm x 13cm)
This English hand-tinted image portrays a nostalgic scene of four children with their cherished toys. A jointed mohair teddy bear, an illustrated book of *Sleeping Beauty*, a character baby, and a handsome horse with cart are represented in this early 20th century commercial real photo postcard. *Anita Johnson Collection.*

I have had playmates,
I have had companions,
In my days of childhood,
In my joyful school days.

Charles Lamb

Fig. 62
8¼in x 5¼in (21cm x 13cm)
This 1925 class photo shows 12 girls who brought their favorite bisque and composition dolls for this special event. However, this unique silver print also pictures one girl (front row, 3rd from left) who dared to be different and brought her cherished dressed teddy bear instead.

Fig. 63 (below)
3¼in x 5¼in (8cm x 13cm)
A little girl in a double-breasted curly mohair "bearskin" coat stands on a photographer's fancy wicker settee in this real photo postcard with a circa 1910 stamp box.

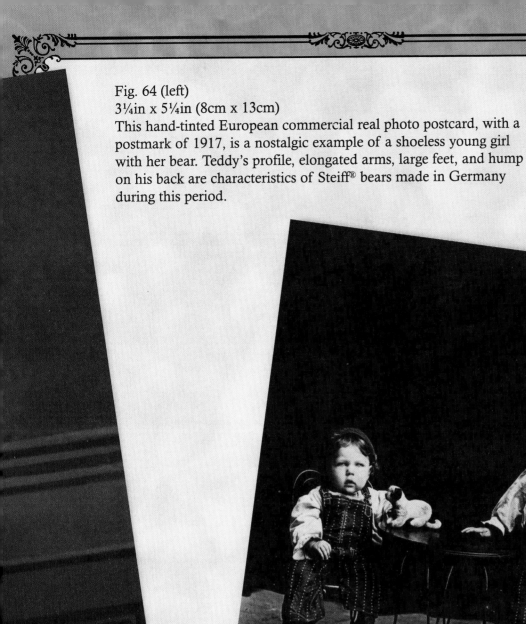

Fig. 64 (left)
3¼in x 5¼in (8cm x 13cm)
This hand-tinted European commercial real photo postcard, with a postmark of 1917, is a nostalgic example of a shoeless young girl with her bear. Teddy's profile, elongated arms, large feet, and hump on his back are characteristics of Steiff® bears made in Germany during this period.

Fig. 65 (above)
3½in x 5½in (9cm x 14cm)
Two boys in matching patterned overalls and caps pose with their small plush dog and rubber ball in this pre-World War I real photo postcard.

Fig. 66 (left)
3½in x 5½in (9cm x 14cm)
This real photo postcard, with a circa 1910 stamp box, is of a girl and her teddy doll with a face probably made of celluloid and a jointed bear-like body of mohair. The head is covered with a fur hood.

Fig. 67 (right)
3¼in x 5¼in (8cm x 13cm)
A white mohair "bearskin" coat along with knit cap, big silk bows, and mittens on a cord make this an unforgettable image of a small girl. This studio real photo postcard has a circa 1915 stamp box.

Fig. 68
4in x 5¾in (10cm x 15cm)
The teddy in this studio silver print of the 1920s resembles the "U.S. stick bear"
with his straight legs, short arms, and sausage-shaped body. The forgotten
American factories that made these bears had no labels attached for identification.
Jim and Janet Doud Collection.

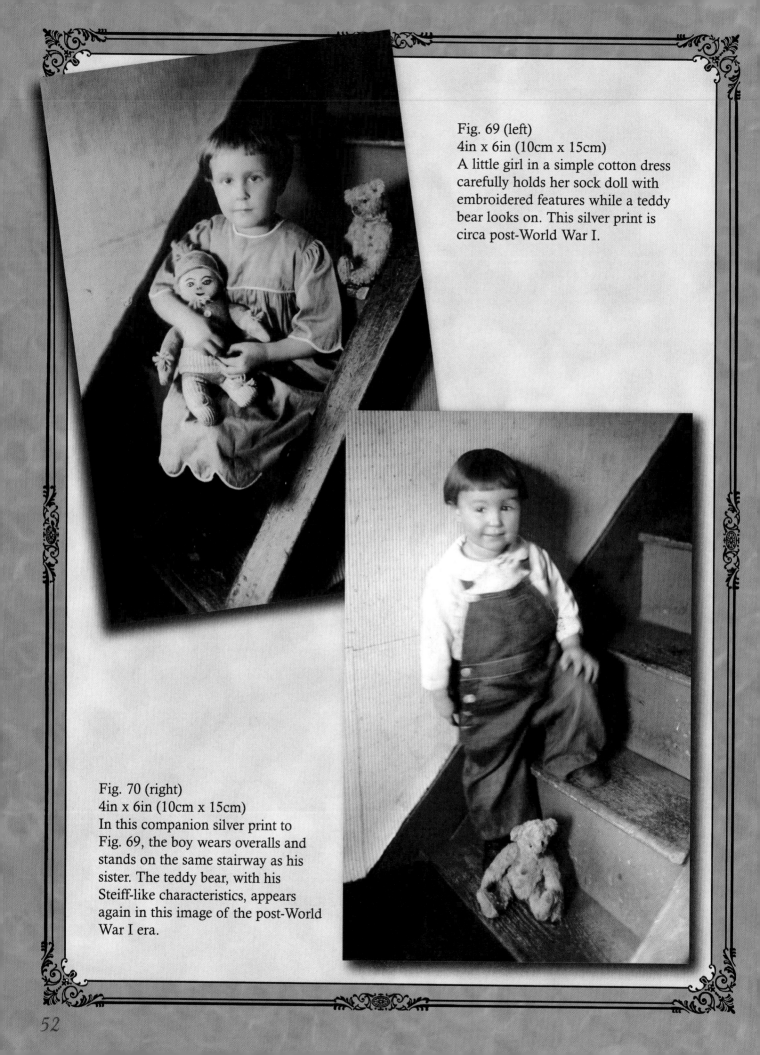

Fig. 69 (left)
4in x 6in (10cm x 15cm)
A little girl in a simple cotton dress carefully holds her sock doll with embroidered features while a teddy bear looks on. This silver print is circa post-World War I.

Fig. 70 (right)
4in x 6in (10cm x 15cm)
In this companion silver print to Fig. 69, the boy wears overalls and stands on the same stairway as his sister. The teddy bear, with his Steiff-like characteristics, appears again in this image of the post-World War I era.

Fig. 71
6in x 4in (15cm x 10cm)
One twin holds a mohair dog puppet, while the other holds a composition doll and a block. They flank their brother on a large wicker settee in this 1920s silver print portrait.

... *"Heaven's first darling, twin born with the morning light, you have floated down the stream of the world's life, and at last you have stranded on my heart.*

As I gaze on your face, mystery overwhelms me; you who belong to all have become mine.

For fear of losing you I hold you tight to my breast. What magic has snared the world's treasure in these slender arms of mine?"

From
"The Beginning"
Rabindranath Tagore
The Crescent Moon

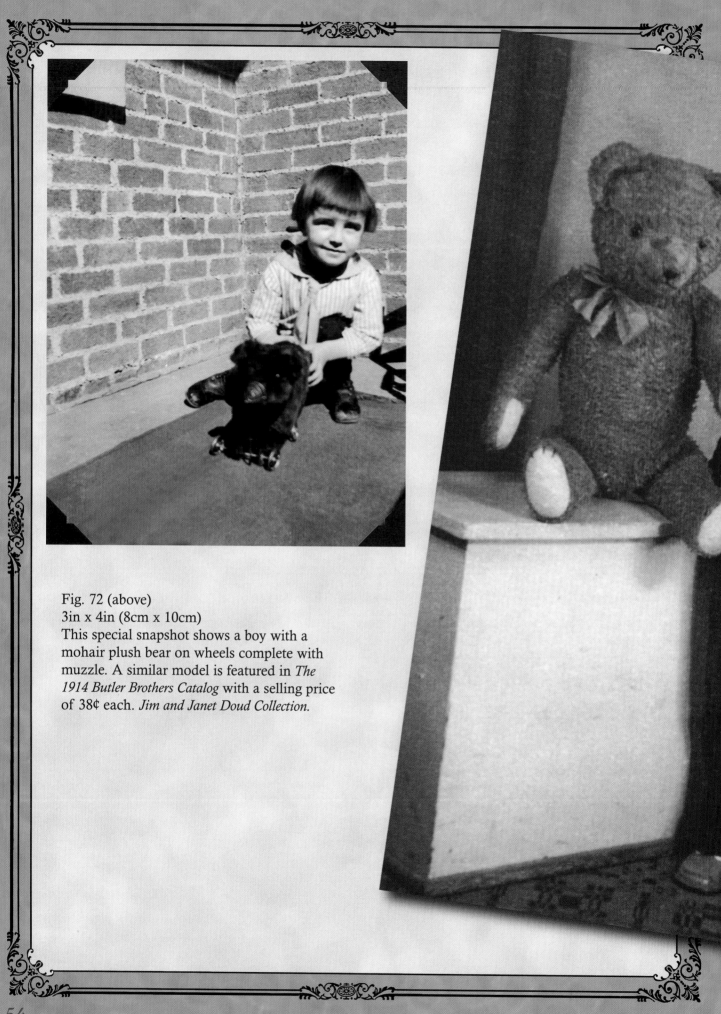

Fig. 72 (above)
3in x 4in (8cm x 10cm)
This special snapshot shows a boy with a
mohair plush bear on wheels complete with
muzzle. A similar model is featured in *The
1914 Butler Brothers Catalog* with a selling price
of 38¢ each. *Jim and Janet Doud Collection.*

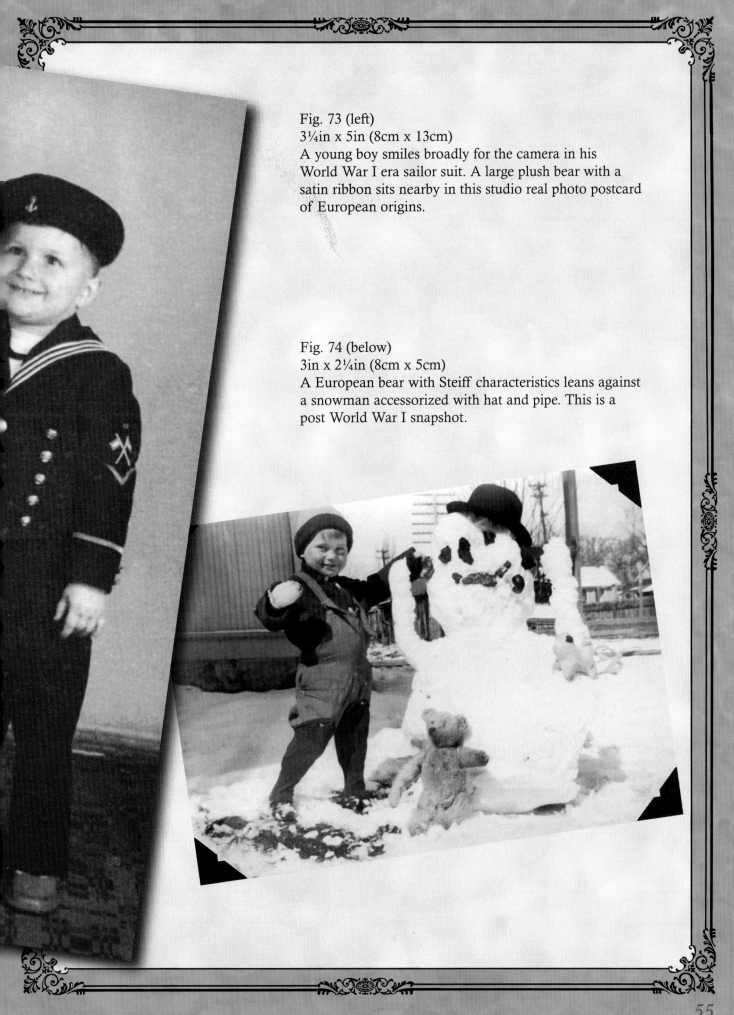

Fig. 73 (left)
3¼in x 5in (8cm x 13cm)
A young boy smiles broadly for the camera in his
World War I era sailor suit. A large plush bear with a
satin ribbon sits nearby in this studio real photo postcard
of European origins.

Fig. 74 (below)
3in x 2¼in (8cm x 5cm)
A European bear with Steiff characteristics leans against
a snowman accessorized with hat and pipe. This is a
post World War I snapshot.

Fig. 75
3½in x 5½in (9cm x 14cm)
A Parisian pink-tinted commercial real photo postcard of the 1920's features a
stylish young miss in her white rabbit fur coat and turban style hat inspired by
the American film star, Clara Bow.

Fig. 76 (left)
3½in x 5½in (9cm x 14cm)
A baby with a white embroidered eyelet collar sits on a fur rug in this real photo postcard of the early 20th century. A jointed white mohair bear of European origins watches by his side.

Fig. 77 (below)
3½in x 3½in (9cm x 9cm)
Mimi stands proudly with her doll she has named "Mary", a large hard plastic American made doll of the 1950s. John poses with a stuffed monkey made of socks and his molded "fire-dog" in this candid snapshot. *Mimi Dietrich Collection.*

Fig. 78 (left)
3½in x 5½in (9cm x 14cm)
This real photo postcard dated 1913
shows a toddler dressed in her
Sunday best coat and bonnet with
fancy satin ruching. The origin of
the bear is unknown, however he
has characteristics of a teddy bear
made by a quality manufacturer.

Fig. 79 (right)
3¼in x 5¼in (8cm x 13cm)
This French hand-tinted commercial
real photo postcard is of a startled
baby seated on a decorated chamber
pot. A jointed beige mohair bear is
nearby in this image from the early
20th century.

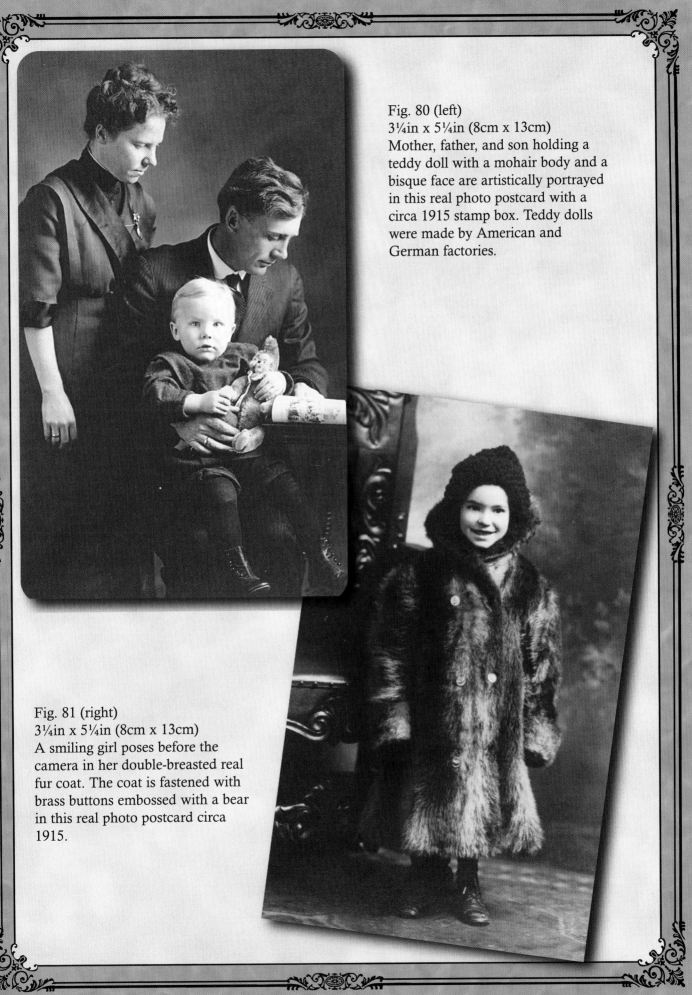

Fig. 80 (left)
3¼in x 5¼in (8cm x 13cm)
Mother, father, and son holding a teddy doll with a mohair body and a bisque face are artistically portrayed in this real photo postcard with a circa 1915 stamp box. Teddy dolls were made by American and German factories.

Fig. 81 (right)
3¼in x 5¼in (8cm x 13cm)
A smiling girl poses before the camera in her double-breasted real fur coat. The coat is fastened with brass buttons embossed with a bear in this real photo postcard circa 1915.

...It makes us all feel good to have a
    baby on the place,
With his everlasten crowing and his
    dimpling, dumpling face.
The patter of his pinky feet makes
    music everywhere,
And when he shakes those fists of his,
    good bye to every care!
No matter what our trouble is when he
    begins to coo,
Old gran'ma laughs,
And gran'pa laughs
Wife, she laughs
And I - you bet, I laugh, too!

From
"The Happy Household"
Eugene Field
Poems of Childhood

Fig. 82 (above)
4in x 6in (10cm x 15cm)
A baby dressed in white holds an
unusual stuffed squirrel and wears
button shoes in this circa 1910 silver
print.

Fig. 83 (left)
3½in x 5½in (9cm x 14cm)
A young girl wearing her dress-up bow and Sunday shoes proudly holds her teddy in this real photo postcard. This bear has large ears sewn down the sides of his head, a black triangular nose, and slightly pointed feet. These are characteristics of bears made by the Ideal Novelty and Toy Company before World War I in United States.

Fig. 84 (below)
7in x 3½in (18cm x 9cm)
With the caption "When Teddy faces Teddy, it means Death or Glory," this albumen stereograph image is dated 1908. This endearing playtime scene was photographed during the teddy craze.
Jim and Janet Doud Collection.

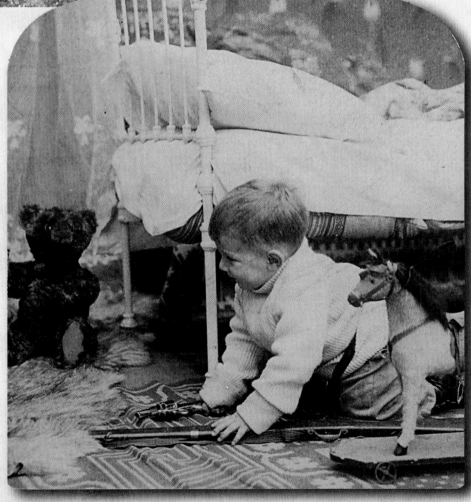

Fig. 85 (left)
3½in x 5in (9cm x 13cm)
This rare real photo postcard from the 1920s shows a very large bear on wheels with a small girl leaning over its broad back. This example is very similar to Steiff® models produced in Germany during this period.

Fig. 86 (right)
3½in x 5½in (9cm x 14cm)
A European real photo postcard dated 1920 captures the image of a happy toddler boy holding the paw of a large mohair teddy bear.

Fig. 87 (left)
3in x 4in (8cm x 10cm)
This World War I era studio silver print is an image of a baby wearing a fluffy coat with matching hat trimmed with ribbon rosettes.

Fig. 88 (right)
3½in x 5½in (9cm x 14cm)
A green velvet poke bonnet trimmed with fur frames the face of a young girl in this European tinted real photo postcard printed in the first decade of the 20th century. Her muff and collar are white angora.

Fig. 89 (right)
3½in x 5in (9cm x 13cm)
A baby holds a stuffed white angora poodle in this real photo postcard with a circa 1915 stamp box. An older brother holds a paper lithographed picture block. *Jim and Janet Doud Collection.*

Fig. 90 (left)
3½in x 5½in (9cm x 14cm)
This commercial color photomechanical halftone, printed in Germany and postmarked 1913, is a pleasant image of a young girl with a bear, a doll, and a stuffed cloth elephant. *Jim and Janet Doud Collection.*

Fig. 91
3½in x 5½in (9cm x 14cm)
A toddler with a pouting expression poses near a jointed mohair
bear in this real photo postcard with a circa 1915 stamp box.

Fig. 92
6¼in x 4¼in (16cm x 11cm)
The bear in this studio silver print of the World War I era is distinctive with his very
large ears. One girl holds a book and the other holds a doll of undetermined material.
Jim and Janet Doud Collection.

Two good little children, named Mary and
    Ann,
Both happily live, as good girls can;
And though they are not either sullen or mute,
They seldom or never are heard to dispute...

...Whatever occurs, in their work or their play,
They are willing to yield, and give up their own
    way:
Then now let us try their example to mind,
And always, like them, be obliging and kind.

From
"The Good-Natured Girls"
Jane Taylor
Little Ann and Other Poems

Fig. 93 (below)
3in x 5in (8cm x 13cm)
A baby squints at the photographer as he sits on a porch step in his romper suit with a stuffed black and white puppy seated nearby. This snapshot is captioned "My First Pants" and dates during the second decade of the 20th century.

Gelukki
Nieu

Fig. 94 (left)
3¼in x 5¼in (8cm x 13cm)
This French commercial hand-tinted real photo postcard
is a wonderful image of a young girl of the early 1920s
holding a large jointed mohair bear of European origins.

Fig. 95 (above)
3¼in x 5¼in (8cm x 13cm)
A smiling girl poses daintily before the camera in her white
mohair "bearskin" coat with a fleece muff. Her fancy bonnet
is lavishly trimmed with silk bows and lace in this real photo
postcard with a circa 1915 stamp box.

Fig. 96 (right)
3½in x 5½in (9cm x 14cm)
The teddy doll in this real photo
postcard, with a circa 1915 stamp
box, is held by a young girl wearing
a checked gingham allover apron.
The teddy doll is considered rare in
collector circles.

Fig. 97 (left)
3in x 4½in (8cm x 12cm)
A toddler girl poses in her snowsuit
and fur-trimmed bonnet as she
happily shows the camera her
unusual white fur muff with an
attached doll's head. The face of
the doll in this dated 1937 snapshot has large round googly eyes.

Fig. 98
3½in x 5in (9cm x 13cm)
The baby in this studio silver print carefully holds what appears to be a Steiff
bear made of dark brown mohair. Teddy's small cupped ears, shoe button eyes,
and triangular nose indicate a pre-World War I date of origin.

Fig. 99 (left)
3¼in x 4¼in (8cm x 11cm)
A boy with golden curls stands before a photographer's hand-painted backdrop in his overalls and sailor middy top. He holds a jointed mohair bear in this silver print of the early 20th century.

Fig. 100 (below)
5½in x 3½in (14cm x 9cm)
Three stylish young ladies play dress-up in this real photo postcard with a circa 1910 stamp box. Fancy hats, long dresses, and handbags make fashionable outfits as they pose with two Steiff-type bears and a doll.
Jim and Janet Doud Collection.

Fig. 101 (right)
3½in x 5½in (9cm x 14cm)
Three children stand in a stair step pose and give the camera their undivided attention in this real photo postcard with a circa 1915 stamp box. This photo is unusual because the young boy is holding a plush tiger with stripes. *Jim and Janet Doud Collection.*

...*Tiger, tiger, burning bright*
In the forests of the night,
What immortal hand or eye
Dare frame thy fearful symmetry?

From
"The Tiger"
William Blake

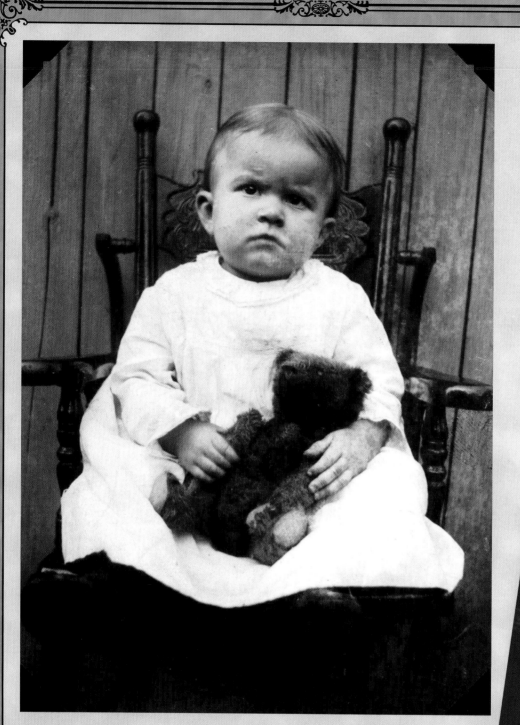

Fig. 102 (above)
3½in x 4¾in (9cm x 12cm)
A scowling baby glares at the camera as he holds a fluffy mohair bear in this silver print with a circa 1912 stamp box. *Jim and Janet Doud Collection.*

Fig. 103 (right)
3½in x 5½in (9cm x 14cm)
This real photo postcard, with a circa 1930 stamp box, shows a toddler boy in a one-piece playsuit happily seated on a wicker bench. His mohair bear with glass eyes is seated close by. *Jim and Janet Doud Collection.*

Fig. 104 (below)
3½in x 5½in (9cm x 14cm)
Two girls pose with their jointed fluffy
mohair bear in this real photo postcard
dated October 30, 1909.

Fig. 105
3¾in x 5½in (10cm x 14cm)
A curly haired toddler dressed in white gazes to the left in a profile view.
Seated nearby, a furry mohair teddy glances at the camera in this World War I
era studio silver print. *Jim and Janet Doud Collection.*

Fig. 106 (left)
2½in x 4in (6cm x 12cm)
A young girl's fluffy angora fur neckpiece and muff are decorated with a grouping of animal heads of unknown origin. Her coat is of corduroy in this endearing post World War I silver print.

Fig. 107 (right)
3½in x 5½in (9cm x 14cm)
A young boy with striped shirt and turquoise suspenders stands near a polar bear and a handsome billy goat. This hand-tinted real photo postcard of French origins is postmarked 1918.

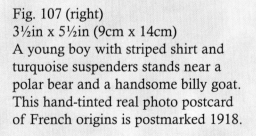

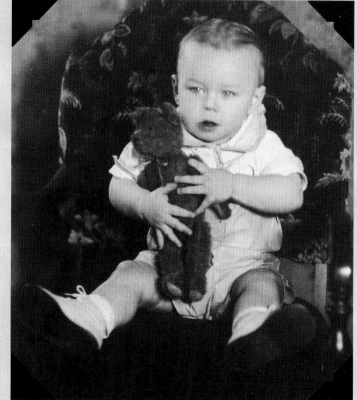

Fig. 108 (above)
3½in x 5½in (9cm x 14cm)
This real photo postcard, with a circa 1915 stamp box, displays a realistic portrayal of two girls in rumpled dresses on their unpainted wood plank porch. Twin bears of short pile wool plush sit in matching perambulators. *Jim and Janet Doud Collection.*

Fig. 109 (right)
3½in x 5in (9cm x 13cm)
In this 1930s silver print, a toddler boy clutches his bear tightly to his chest. The bear's feet are pointed with felt pads.

Fig. 110
3¼in x 5¼in (8cm x 13cm)
A serious young girl in a curly mohair coat and bonnet stands with her
German bisque head doll. Her collar and muff are made from curly
lambs wool trimmed with angora in this real photo postcard with a circa
1915 stamp box. *Jim and Janet Doud Collection.*

Fig. 111
5¼in x 3¼in
(13cm x 8cm)
The two unusual stuffed
felt mice, dressed in their
photo finery, pose with
this large family group.
This real photo postcard
has a circa 1910 stamp
box.

...He rode up to Miss Mousie's door
He rode up to Miss Mousie's door
With his coat all buttoned down before,

He took Miss Mousie on his knee,
He took Miss Mousie on his knee,
And he said my dear will you marry me,

Oh no! Kind sir, I can't say that,
Oh no! Kind sir, I can't say that,
You'll have to get consent of my Uncle Rat,

Uncle Rat he laughed and shook his fat side,
Uncle Rat he laughed and shook his fat side,
To think that his niece would be a bride.

From
"A Frog Went A Courting"
Unknown Author

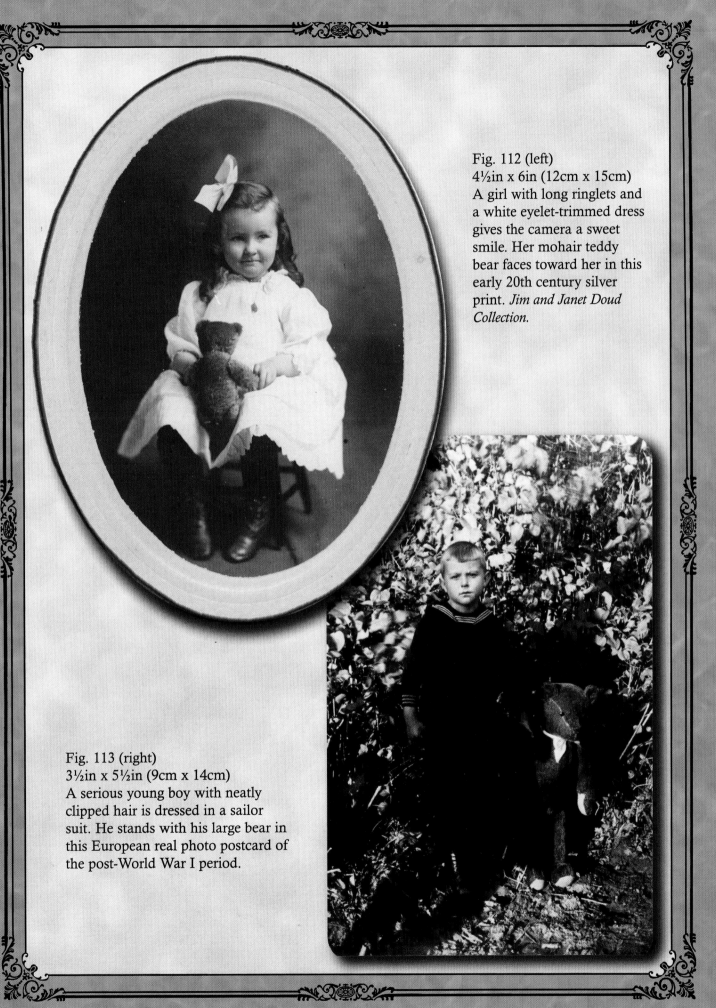

Fig. 112 (left)
4½in x 6in (12cm x 15cm)
A girl with long ringlets and a white eyelet-trimmed dress gives the camera a sweet smile. Her mohair teddy bear faces toward her in this early 20th century silver print. *Jim and Janet Doud Collection.*

Fig. 113 (right)
3½in x 5½in (9cm x 14cm)
A serious young boy with neatly clipped hair is dressed in a sailor suit. He stands with his large bear in this European real photo postcard of the post-World War I period.

Fig. 114 (left)
3½in x 5½in (9cm x 14cm)
The camera has captured the image of a young girl with her costumed teddy bear in this real photo post card of the World War I era.

Fig. 115 (right)
3¼in x 5¼in (8cm x13cm)
This unusual European commercial real photo postcard from the early 20th century depicts a girl in a hand-tinted dress straddling a basket. Inside are two stuffed pigs.

Fig. 116 (left)
3½in x 3½in (9cm x 9cm)
Steven smiles for the camera as he proudly displays his 1950s plush elephant. His brother, Bob, tightly hugs his large plush teddy bear in this candid snapshot.

Fig. 117 (right)
4¼in x 6½in (11cm x 17cm)
A little stuffed dog rests on a Victorian overstuffed chair in this albumen cabinet card dated Christmas 1887. The young child stands pensively nearby in her white dress. *Jim and Janet Doud Collection.*

L. ALMAN.

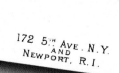

Fig. 118 (right)
3½in x 5½in (9cm x 14cm)
A thoughtful young girl stands before the camera in her mohair "bearskin" coat in this real photo postcard with a circa 1912 stamp box. Her bonnet is trimmed with silk bows and flowers.

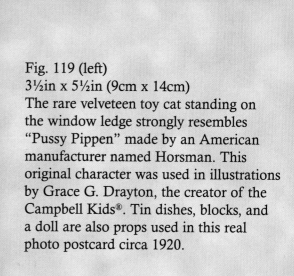

Fig. 119 (left)
3½in x 5½in (9cm x 14cm)
The rare velveteen toy cat standing on the window ledge strongly resembles "Pussy Pippen" made by an American manufacturer named Horsman. This original character was used in illustrations by Grace G. Drayton, the creator of the Campbell Kids®. Tin dishes, blocks, and a doll are also props used in this real photo postcard circa 1920.

Fig. 120
3¾in x 5½in (10cm x 14cm)
A baby sits contentedly with a mohair bear of probable German origins, a cloth camel, and a ball in this studio silver print which is dated 1910. *Jim and Janet Doud Collection.*

Fig. 121
6¾in x 4¾in (17cm x 12cm)
In this silver print from the first decade of the 20th century, four girls pose in the grass for the photographer. The youngest stands with a mohair bear of probable European origins.

Four princesses lived in a Green Tower—
A bright green tower in the middle of the sea;
And no one could think — oh, no one could think—
Who the Four Princesses could be.

One looked to the North, and one to the South
And one to the East, and one to the West;
They were all so pretty, so very pretty,
You could not tell which was the prettiest.

From
"The Four Princesses"
Kate Greenaway
Marigold Garden, 1885

Fig. 122 (above)
3½in x 5½in (9cm x 14cm)
The striking ermine fur collarette and muff contrasts sharply with the girl's dark coat and fancy bonnet in this real photo postcard dated 1911.

Fig. 123 (right)
3½in x 5½in (9cm x 14cm)
This European commercial real photo postcard from the early 1920s is colorfully hand tinted. The girl in green holds a bear tucked under her packages.

Fig. 124 (above)
3in x 6in (8cm x 15cm)
A little boy in his romper suit poses with a sad expression
in this studio silver print of the pre-World War I era. A
white angora poodle dog with a velvet body stands nearby.
Jim and Janet Doud Collection.

Fig. 125 (right)
3½in x 5½in (9cm x 14cm)
This dated 1911 real photo postcard
features two children in their mohair
"bearskin" coats so popular during
this period. The oversized girl's coat
is trimmed with angora and curly
lamb's wool.

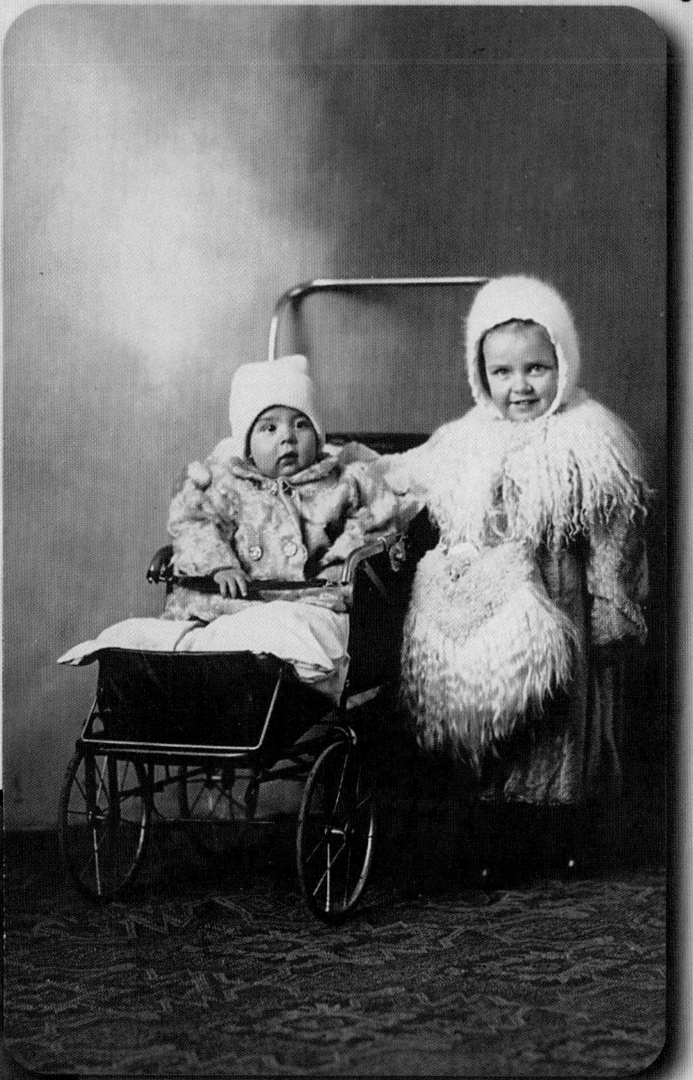

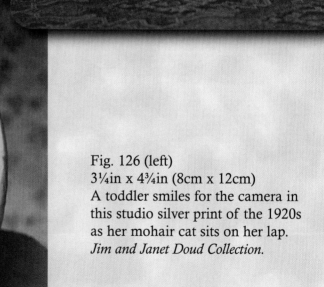

Fig. 126 (left)
3¼in x 4¾in (8cm x 12cm)
A toddler smiles for the camera in
this studio silver print of the 1920s
as her mohair cat sits on her lap.
Jim and Janet Doud Collection.

Fig. 127
4½in x 6in (12cm x 15cm)
A boy clutches his bear under one arm as a baby sits nearby in an infant's long
christening dress with eyelet-trimmed underslip. This studio silver print is of
pre-World War I vintage. *Jim and Janet Doud Collection.*

Fig. 128 (above)
5in x 3½in (13cm x 9cm)
This real photo postcard, with a circa 1915 stamp box, portrays a boy cradling a cat in his lap, a baby strapped in a gocart, and a girl with a white dog. The large teddy bear is probably German and sits on the lap of his mistress.

Fig. 129 (right)
3¼in x 5in (8cm x 13cm)
A handsome European teddy bear with a shaved muzzle sits on an ornate pedestal stand. A girl dressed in a white eyelet dress stands nearby in this pre-World War I real photo postcard.

The Scarlet Coat

Her coat was so scarlet
So bright, oh so red,
Near sugar white snow
As she rode on her sled.

Sliding and gliding
With friends she did ride,
Her coat, oh so scarlet
Was soft warm inside.

Uphill and downhill
All day she did play,
Her coat, oh so scarlet
Kept cold winds away.

M.M. Wikert

Fig. 130
3½in x 5½in (9cm x 14cm)
This brightly hand-tinted European real photo postcard produced commercially in the 1920s depicts an extraordinary array of stuffed toys. A white mohair bear, a felt elephant on metal wheels with Steiff characteristics, a cloth doll with printed googly eyes, and a monkey of probable Steiff origins are all represented.

Fig. 131 (left)
3¼in diameter (8cm diameter)
This trimmed real photo postcard from the post-World War I era depicts a young boy in his overcoat and knit hockey cap gazing down at his mohair bear of possible American manufacture.

Fig. 132 (above)
5½in x 3½in (14cm x 9cm)
A toddler protectively holds a teddy bear as the camera captures the moment in this real photo postcard with a pre-1915 stamp box.

Fig. 133 (right)
3in x 5½in (8cm x 14cm)
The smiles on the faces of
both girl and bear in this
pleasing studio silver print,
dating sometime before
1910, make this an
unforgettable image.
The upturned face of the
bear makes identification
difficult, however he
seems happy that
both he and his
mistress are decked
in bows for the
photographer.
*Jim and Janet Doud
Collection.*

Fig. 134
3in x 5½in (8cm x 14cm)
A fluffy mohair bear gazes up at a toddler wearing a white embroidered eyelet dress with a ruffled bertha collar in this studio silver print taken around World War I.

Fig. 135 (left)
3in x 4¾in (8cm x 12cm)
Two young girls pose in the grass in this snapshot dated 1943. The toddler holds a plush white stuffed animal with printed cloth pants and felt shoes.

Fig. 136 (right)
4¼in x 6¼in (11cm x 16cm)
This albumen cabinet card from the 1890s portrays two girls in their winter outfits each trimmed in white fur. The photographer's elaborate wicker chair is of Victorian design.

Vermont Photo Co.

3599

Fig. 137 (above left)
3½in x 5in (9cm x 13cm)
A little girl smiles spontaneously in this studio silver print as she holds a
toy animal. A bear of probable German origins sits nearby in this circa
1915 photograph. *Jim and Janet Doud Collection.*

Fig. 138 (above right)
5¼in x 3¼in (13cm x 8cm)
A European commercial hand-tinted real photo postcard of the 1920s
features a girl with her mask face fabric doll. Of possible earlier vintage,
a fur-covered donkey with saddle and a wool sheep both have small
metal wheels on their feet.

Fig. 139 (right)
2¼in x 3½in (6cm x 9cm)
A child poses for the camera in this tintype of the 1870s. This image is unusual because of the small stuffed fabric black cat used as a prop. *Jim and Janet Doud Collection.*

Fig. 140 (left)
3½in x 5½in (9cm x 14cm)
The camera has captured the gentle smile of this young girl as she stands in her curled mohair "bearskin" coat, knit cap, and angora muff. This real photo postcard is dated 1909.

Fig. 141 (right)
3¼in x 5¼in (8cm x 13cm)
This real photo postcard from the early 20th century portrays a young girl in a knit double-breasted coat and hockey cap holding a German bear with Steiff characteristics.

Fig. 142 (left)
3½in x 5½in (9cm x 14cm)
A little girl dressed in white with a fancy ribbon-trimmed bonnet stands on a fur rug in this studio real photo postcard postmarked 1908. A mohair bear sits nearby with paws outstretched toward the camera.

Fig. 143 (right)
3½in x 5½in (9cm x 14cm)
This postmarked 1907 real photo postcard depicts a happy young boy in a double-breasted coat with matching Tam O'Shanter cap. The toddler girl wears a curly lamb's wool coat with matching leggings and carries a purse.

Happiness is a Butterfly

"Happiness is a butterfly,
Which, when pursued,
Is always just beyond your
grasp,
But which,
If you will sit down quietly,
May alight upon you."

Nathaniel Hawthorne

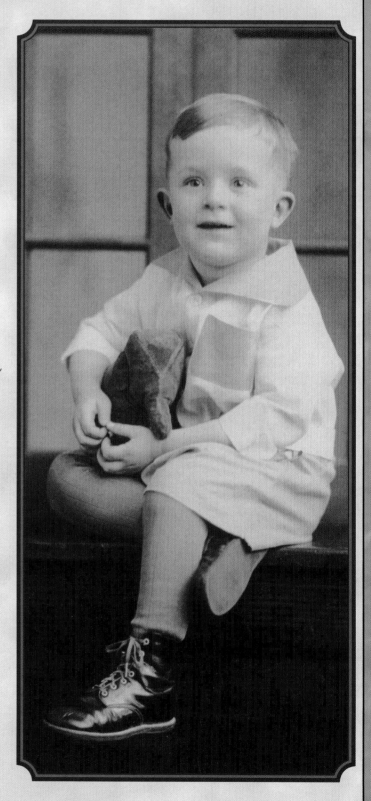

Fig. 144 (right)
4in x 6in (10cm x 15cm)
The camera has captured the sparkle in the eyes of this young boy dressed in a romper suit from the post-World War I era. This studio silver print also shows a stuffed plush elephant tucked under the boy's arm.

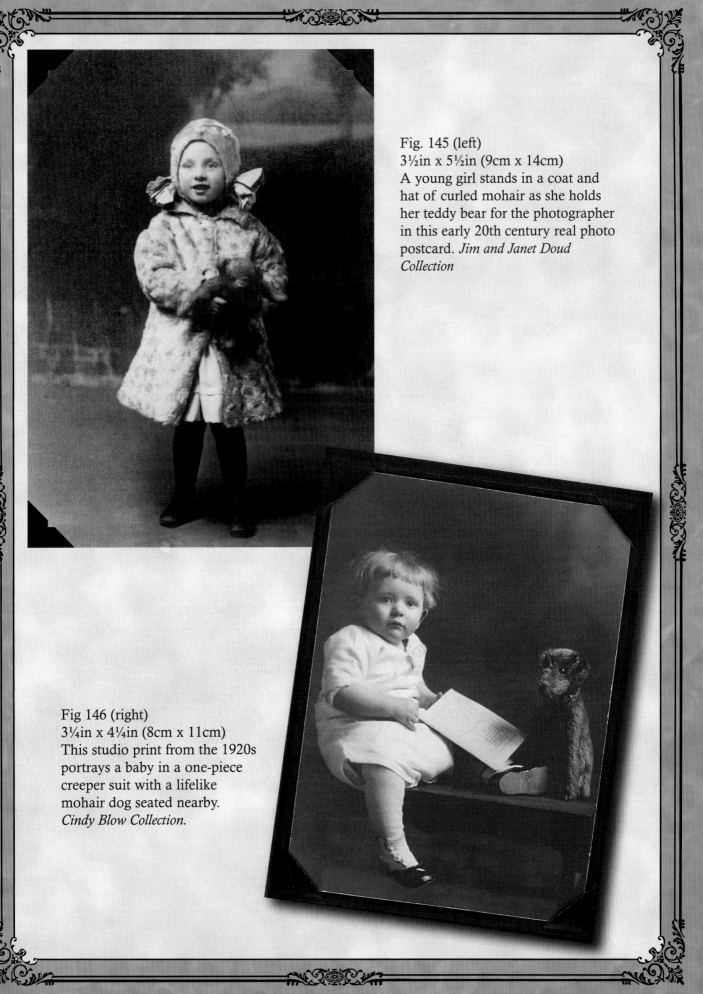

Fig. 145 (left)
3½in x 5½in (9cm x 14cm)
A young girl stands in a coat and hat of curled mohair as she holds her teddy bear for the photographer in this early 20th century real photo postcard. *Jim and Janet Doud Collection*

Fig 146 (right)
3¼in x 4¼in (8cm x 11cm)
This studio print from the 1920s portrays a baby in a one-piece creeper suit with a lifelike mohair dog seated nearby. *Cindy Blow Collection.*

Fig. 147
3½in x 5½in (9cm x 14cm)
A toddler in a striped crocheted dress poses near a very large stuffed cotton elephant
and a cloth doll in this real photo postcard of the World War I era.

Fig. 148 (left)
3½in x 4½in (9cm x 12cm)
In this real photo postcard dated 1909, a girl is wearing a dark coat of glossy mohair with small close curls called astrakhan. Her pointed bonnet, muff-purse combination, and leggings all match her coat in this stylish outfit.

Fig. 149 (right)
3½in x 5½in (9cm x 14cm)
The setting in this real photo postcard postmarked 1908 provides an unusual backdrop for a girl seated in a child-size wood rocker. The bear she holds has Steiff® characteristics. *Cindy Blow Collection.*

Fig. 150 (above)
2½in x 4in (6cm x 10cm)
The "bearskin" fluffy coat is unusual in this studio silver print of the early 20th century. The mohair has been sheared to create an all over pattern that is readily visible as the toddler leans over a child-size ice cream chair.

Fig. 151 (left)
3¼in x 5¼in (8cm x 13cm)
This candid real photo
postcard of the 1920s
shows a girl with her
large teddy bear. The
sausage-shaped body,
short stubby arms, and
stiff legs with small feet
are clues that this bear is
of possible American
manufacture.

Fig. 152 (above)
3½in x 6in (9cm x 15cm)
The white mohair oversized "bearskin" coat is fastened with corded
"frogs" in this studio silver print of the early 20th century. Large
silk bows accent the cap of this fair-haired child.

The End

Fig. 153 (above)
5½in x 3½in (14 cm x 9cm)
"Surprise!" is the best word to describe this candid snapshot of a baby and her much loved fleece lamb taken during the early 20th century.

Fig. 154 (right)
3½ in x 3½ in (9cm x 9cm)
This final image is a rare snapshot circa 1930-1940 of a child photographer at work with her box camera. Her most worthy subject is a handsome fluffy mohair bear with a clipped muzzle.

Guide to Photographic Terms

The **Daguerreotype** was introduced in France by Louis Daguerre in 1839 and was the first practical photographic process. The image was developed by a complicated single image process on a silver coated copper plate. These cased images lost favor by 1860 and are identified by a mirror image when held at an angle.

The **Ambrotype**, invented by Frederick Scott Archer of England in 1841 and patented by James Ambrose Cutting in the United States in 1844, was a cased negative image made with the wet-plate process on a glass surface. This fragile negative image was viewed as positive when a black backing was added. No copies could be made once the backing was applied. Last produced in 1865, the ambrotype is identified by the absence of a reflective mirror image when compared to the daguerreotype.

The **Tintype**, (also called melainotype or ferrotype) was patented in 1856 by an American, Hannibal Smith. Tintype production was similar to that of the ambrotype with one exception—a thin iron sheet was utilized rather than a glass plate. No copies could be made, but a multi-lens camera allowed duplicates of the image to be taken in one sitting. The popular, durable, and inexpensive tintype was produced into the 20th century, although cased images were made only until 1868. Identification of a cased tintype can be made with a magnet against the glass or when possible, with removal from the case.

The **Image Case**, introduced in 1839, served as a protector for daguerreotypes, ambrotypes and tintypes. Wood frame cases were covered with embossed leather, cardboard, or papier-mâché, while others were molded thermoplastic cases. Some were further decorated with paintings, gilding, or inlays of tortoiseshell or mother-of-pearl. The image case lost favor by the late 1860s.

The **Albumen Print**, invented by Louis-Désiré Blanquart-Evrard in 1850, was a positive image produced from a glass plate negative (wet-plate process) on sensitized paper coated with egg whites. Multiple copies were possible from the glass plate negative. Examples of mounted albumen print formats included the carte de visite, cabinet card, and stereograph. Albumen prints can be identified by fading, yellowing, staining, foxing (brown spots from mold or impurities) and surface crazing.

The **Carte de Visite** was introduced in France by André-Adolphe Eugène-Disdéri in 1854. This small albumen print mounted on cardboard stock (2½in x 4in) was the size of a Victorian calling or visiting card. Small "gem" tintypes were also used in this format after being placed in decorative paper sleeves. The idea of a family album became popular with the affordable and accessible carte de visite. By 1870, its popularity waned with the advent of the cabinet card.

The **Cabinet Card** was developed in 1863 by the London Studios of Windsor & Bridge. Most cabinet cards were albumen prints mounted on cardboard stock (4¼in x 6½in). Bigger albums were required to accommodate this Victorian format, popular between 1870-1900. Many photographers lavishly printed their names on the front and back in elaborate script.

The **Stereograph** was a set of two photographs taken of the same subject from slightly different perspectives. When mounted side-by-side on a cardboard backing and observed through a hand held stereoscope, an image of a three dimensional picture was created. An Englishman, Sir Charles Brewster, invented the stereoscope in 1849. The most common form is the albumen print (1850-1900). Stereograph dating can be determined by the shape and color of the card mount and by the type of photographic process used.

The **Cyanotype**, developed by Sir John Herschel in the 1840s, was a photographic image much like the modern blue print. Popular with amateur photographers from 1890-1910, cyanotypes were primarily used as artist's proofs. Cyanotypes are identified by their distinctive blue color.

The **Silver Print** is a loosely encompassing contemporary term describing paper prints made after the invention of gelatin coated paper in the 1880s. Silver, an important component of the gelatin, helped to produce a photo-sensitive surface on the paper. Many early prints may be identified by silver mirroring, a shiny bluish metallic sheen found on the edges and shadow areas of the image.

The **Real Photo Postcard** was an actual photograph printed on postcard-size stock (usually 3½in x 5½in) from a camera's negative. Examples from 1900 to 1906 had space on the front for messages, while postcards after 1907 allowed space for messages on the back. Studying the preprinted lettering styles and the stamp box design (the rectangular space for the stamp) on the back of a postcard helps to date an image from 1905-1950.

Photomechanical Reproduction Processes were used by commercial manufacturers to reproduce photographs with a printing press and ink. These processes were less expensive and time consuming than actual photographic printing on light sensitive paper. With the aid of a magnifying glass, collotypes, photogravures, and halftones are easily identified by the presence of dots, lines, curvy shaped patterns, irregular graining, and no fading. In contrast, a real photo will have clarity with no patterns and some degree of fading is usually evident.

Selected Bibliography

American Teddy Bear Encyclopedia, by Linda Mullins (Hobby House Press, Grantsville, Maryland, 1995).

American Victorian Costume in Early Photographs, by Priscilla Harris Dalrymple (Dover Publications, Mineola, New York, 1991).

Antique Children's Fashions: 1880-1900, by Hazel Ulseth and Helen Shannon (Hobby House Press, Cumberland, Maryland, 1983).

Boy's Fashions: 1885 to 1905 Chronicle for Costume Historians and Doll Costumers, compiled by Donna H. Felger (Hobby House Press, Cumberland, Maryland, 1984).

The Camera and Its Images, by Arthur Goldsmith (Newsweek Books, New York, New York, 1979).

Care and Identification of 19th Century Photographic Prints, by James M. Reilly (Eastman Kodak Co., 1986).

Collector's Guide to Early Photographs, by O. Henry Mace (Wallace-Homestead Book Company, Radnor, Pennsylvania, 1990).

Dressed for the Photographer: Ordinary Americans and Fashion 1840-1900, by Joan Severa (Kent State University Press, Kent, Ohio, 1995).

4th Teddy Bear and Friends Price Guide, by Linda Mullins (Hobby House Press, Cumberland, Maryland, 1993).

History of Photography, by Beaumont Newhall (Museum of Modern Art, New York, New York, 1982).

Keepers of Light, by William Crawford (Morgan and Morgan, Dobbs Ferry, New York, 1979).

The Picture History of Photography: From the Earliest Beginnings to the Present Day, by Peter Pollack (H.N. Abrams, New York, New York, 1969).

Prairie Fires and Paper Moons: The American Photographic Postcard, 1900-1920, by Hale Morgan and Andreas Brown (David R. Godine, Boston, Massachusetts, 1981).

Second Edition Collector's Guide to Early Photographs, by O. Henry Mace (Krause Publications, Iola, Wisconsin, 1999).

Steiff Teddy Bears, Dolls, and Toys, by Jean Wilson and Shirley Conway (Wallace Homestead, West Des Moines, Iowa, 1984).

The Teddy Bear Encyclopedia, by Pauline Cockrill (Dorling, Kindersley, New York, New York, 1993).

Teddy Bears Past and Present: A Collector's Guide by Linda Mullins (Hobby House Press, Cumberland, Maryland, 1986).

Teddy Bears and Steiff Animals, by Margaret Fox Mandel (Collector's Books, Paducah, Kentucky, 1984).

Victorian and Edwardian Fashion: A Photographic Survey, by Alison Gernsheim (Dover Publications, New York, New York, 1981).

Victorian and Edwardian Photographs, by Margaret Harker (7 Hills Books, 1982).

Photographic Attributions

Figure numbers not listed denote origins unknown. **1:** The Wykeham Studios Ltd., 304 High Holborn, Balham, Streatham. **3:** Warren & Parsons, Spirit Lake, Ia. **6:** Noyer in circle symbol/1765, Photographic Véritable, Printed in France. **10:** GG Co., 1809/6. **11:** Illegible logo, 63376/3. **13:** Willyerd, Bryan, Texas. **14:** Pollard Graham & Son, Derby, Northampton, Kettering & Wellingborough. **18:** A.N. Paris, 487. **19:** Van Ralty Studios-Manchester, Liverpool, Sheffield, Nottingham, Oldham, Bolton. **25:** Patten Bros., Waterloo, Wis. **28:** Hand, torch, and bird symbol, 511/3. **34:** New York Art Gallery, Holdridge's Block, Janesville, Wis. **35:** CB in symbol, Paris, 1145. **38:** Illegible logo. **44:** E.W. White, 292 Harrison Ave., Detroit, Mich. **46:** Palmer, Griggsville, Ills. **47:** Noyer in circle symbol, 1259, Made in France. **49:** Illegible logo. **51:** Harper, Audobon, IA. **54:** John Esmay, Landscape & Portrait Photographer, Sabula, Iowa. **55:** Hallett & Brother, 134 & 136 Bowery, Near Grand Street, NY. **57:** Kelly's Studio, Oskaloosa, IA. **59:** Anshutz Studio, Keokuk, IA. **61:** Marcuse Day & Co. Ltd., London E.O., printed in Prussia. **62:** Francis Thompson Studio, San Francisco. **64:** GL Co. symbol 4743/4. **73:** Illegible logo. **75:** P.C. Paris in circle symbol, 3112, Diamont, G.E.F. **76:** Illegible logo. **77:** Mimi Dietrich family photograph. **79:** CB in symbol, Paris 650. **81:** Forseen, Opera House Block, St. Paul. **84:** Underwood & Underwood, Publishers, New York, London, Toronto-Canada, Ottawa-Kansas, Works and Studios, Arlington, N.J., Westwood, N.J. **88:** Illegible symbol and signature, S477-5242. **90:** 1439/5, Printed in Germany. **94:** RIP 1337, Made in France. **98:** Lewis, Utica, N.Y. **103:** Stauts Waco. **107:** Furia 635/2. **108:** Brady Brothers, Kansas City, Mo. **115:** n 1649. **116:** Steven Wikert family photograph. **117:** L. Alman, 172 5th Ave., N.Y. and Newport, R.I. **119:** Letcher, Dodgeville, Wis. **123:** CEKO symbol, 1554. **128:** E. Straus, 1426 Wash. Ave., So., Minneapolis, Minn. **129:** Henri Solomon, (late with Lafayette), Studios: 22 Lombard St., Belfast. **130:** CEKO symbol, 1562. **134:** Elarton Studio, Aurora, Nebr. **136:** Vermont Photo Co. **138:** RTB in circle symbol, 3599. **141:** J.P. Bamber, 69 Church St., Blackpool, 171. Lord St., Southport. **146:** Illegible logo. **150:** The Barkhurst Studio, opposite Post Office, Beatrice, Neb.

Other Books In This Series Include:

Cherish Me Always: A Century of Dolls
Cherish Me Always: Animal Friends (Spring 2002 release)
Cherish Me Always: Images of Christmas Past (Fall 2002 release)

About the Authors

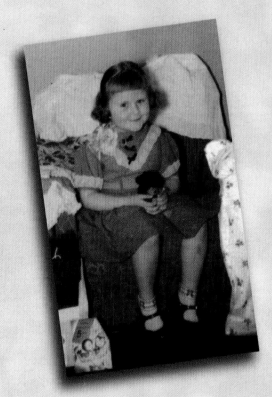

Mary McMurray Wikert

Mary was raised and educated in the Midwest, graduating from the University of Iowa with a degree in arts education. She has taught thousands of students on all grade levels in her art position with the public schools. Mary has completed additional graduate work and research, and feels her strongest emphasis and interests are in the areas of art history, costume design, illustrative drawing, and the decorative arts. She is a past president and a member of a nationally federated doll club and is a knowledgeable doll historian. Her intense interest in historical photographs grew from her love for antique dolls and toys. Raising two sons in Cedar Falls, Iowa, with her husband, Steve, has strengthened her convictions of preserving images of children with the things they cherish.

Steven Micheal Wikert

Steve, who was formerly a municipal cultural director, is now an arts educator in the public schools, a visual artist, a knowledgeable photographer, and a published poet. He was raised in Iowa and returned there after his service in the U. S. Navy and Vietnam. Studying arts education, public relations, and educational administration, he has earned a BA, an MA, and an Advanced Studies Certificate from the University of Northern Iowa. He and his wife, Mary, have raised two sons in Cedar Falls, Iowa. He has a love for vintage teddy bears and many other antiques. His personal/professional background and his many years of collecting antique photographs, have heightened Steve's ability to discover quality images of children with the things they cherish.